A Note to Parents

W9-BZO-531

For many children, learning math is difficult and "I hate math!" is their first response — to which many parents silently add "Me, too!" Children often see adults comfortably reading and writing, but they rarely have such models for mathematics. And math fear can be catching!

The easy-to-read stories in this **Hello Reader! Math** series were written to give children a positive introduction to mathematics, and parents a pleasurable re-acquaintance with a subject that is important to everyone's life. **Hello Reader! Math** stories make mathematical ideas accessible, interesting, and fun for children. The activities and suggestions at the end of each book provide parents with a hands-on approach to help children develop mathematical interest and confidence.

Enjoy the mathematics!
• Give your child a chance to retell the story. The more familiar children are with the story, the more they will understand its mathematical concepts.
• Use the colorful illustrations to help children "hear and see" the math at work in the story.
• Treat the math activities as games to be played for fun. Follow your child's lead. Spend time on those activities that engage your child's interest and curiosity.
• Activities, especially ones using physical materials, help make abstract mathematical ideas concrete.

Learning is a messy process. Learning about math calls for children to become immersed in lively experiences that help them make sense of mathematical concepts and symbols.

Although learning about numbers is basic to math, other ideas, such as identifying shapes and patterns, measuring, collecting and interpreting data, reasoning logically, and thinking about chance, are also important. By reading these stories and having fun with the activities, you will help your child enthusiastically say "**Hello, math,**" instead of "I hate math."

—Marilyn Burns
National Mathematics Educator
Author of *The I Hate Mathematics! Book*

To Roxy
— D.O.

To Rosie, my little inspiration
— M.D.

No part of this publication may be reproduced in whole or in part, or stored in a retrieval system, or transmitted in any form or by any means, electronic, mechanical, photocopying, recording, or otherwise, without written permission of the publisher. For information regarding permissions, write to Scholastic Inc., Attention: Permissions Department, 555 Broadway, New York, NY 10012.

Copyright © 1998 by Scholastic Inc.
The activities on pages 35-40 copyright © 1998 by Marilyn Burns.
All rights reserved. Published by Scholastic Inc.
SCHOLASTIC, HELLO READER! and CARTWHEEL BOOKS and associated logos
are trademarks and/or registered trademarks of Scholastic Inc.

Library of Congress Cataloging-in-Publication Data
Ochiltree, Dianne.
    Cats add up! / by Diane Ochiltree; illustrated by Marcy Dunn-Ramsey;
math activities by Marilyn Burns.
        p.   cm.—(Hello reader! Math. Level 3)
    Summary: A family with one cat keeps adding more until they give some of the
cats away. Includes related activities.
    ISBN 0-590-12005-0
    [1. Cats—Fiction. 2. Counting.] I. Ramsey, Marcy Dunn, ill.
II. Burns, Marilyn. III. Title. IV. Series.
PZ7.0165Cat   1998
[E]—dc21   97-43659
                                                                              CIP
                                                                              AC

10 9 8 7 6 5 4 3 2 1   8 9/9 0/0 01 02
                        Printed in the U.S.A.   24
                        First printing, October 1998

Cats Add Up!

by Dianne Ochiltree
Illustrated by Marcy Dunn-Ramsey
Math Activities by Marilyn Burns

Hello Reader! Math — Level 3

SCHOLASTIC INC.
New York   Toronto   London   Auckland   Sydney

Mama always says,
"One is just the right number of cats for us."

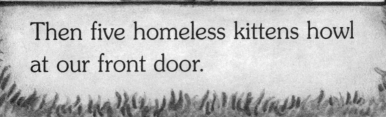

Then five homeless kittens howl
at our front door.

Our cat Maxie sniffs them
and swishes her tail.
I name them Bongo, Pepper, Stripe,
Muffin, and Blue.
Five kittens and our cat Maxie
add up to six.

Mama says, "Six cats is five too many.
One was just the right number."

Then our neighbor moves to a place with a sign that says: NO CATS!
So Whiskers and Sam come to live with us. Two old cats and five kittens and our cat Maxie add up to eight.

Mama says, "Eight cats is seven too many. One was just the right number."

But one day a stray cat hops into
my backpack.
Cat Fish has long whiskers that bounce up
and down on the bus ride home.

One stray cat and two old cats and five
kittens and our cat Maxie add up to nine.

Mama says, "Nine cats is eight too many.
One was just the right number."

Then something scoots through the door
behind her.

Scooty pokes his nose inside the
shopping bags.
He pushes boxes off the table.

Then he rubs Mama's foot and curls
around her leg.
Mama sighs. She looks at the ten cats.
I know what she is thinking.
But Mama just says, "We'll see."

Now twenty cat eyes open wide and watch Mama cook.

Ten tails disappear when Mama makes the bed.

Twenty ears shoot up when a dog barks.
Forty paws scratch Mama's new chair.

Ten cats leap into the clothes basket.
Ten cats wiggle out.

Ten cats hiss at another ten cats hiding in the hall, and ten cats get sticky whiskers when Mama turns her back.

Mama's nose starts to twitch.
Her eyes begin to itch.
First it's just a sneeze.
Then it's a wheeze.
"Ten cats is too many!" Mama says.

I put signs up everywhere:
FREE CATS. All colors, all sizes, all cute.
Get yours today!

Mrs. Minnow takes Bongo to be a watch
cat in her store.
Bongo gets paid all the fish she can eat.

One cat taken away from ten is nine.

Our new neighbor takes Whiskers and Sam to help her sort balls of yarn.

Two cats taken away from nine is seven.

The Wilson triplets take Pepper, Muffin,
and Blue.
They always get three of everything.

Three cats taken away from seven is four.

A farmer takes Cat Fish and Stripe to work in his barn.

He says they look mean enough to scare the mice, but not the cows.

Two cats taken away from four is two.

A truck driver takes Scooty.
They hit the road together.

One cat taken away from
two is one.

Now Mama stops wheezing and sneezing.
"See," she says,
"one is just the right
number of cats for us."

And it was, until . . .

. . . Maxie had four kittens!

And what do you think Mama said about *that*?

• ABOUT THE ACTIVITIES •

Learning addition and subtraction combinations is standard in the early grades in school. However, developing number sense is also extremely important for young children. Children with strong number sense have good intuition about numbers and an "I can do" attitude toward solving problems with numbers. They understand how numbers relate to one another, show flexibility in thinking about and working with numbers, and can apply what they know to new situations.

Cats Add Up! is an engaging story that gives children the chance to think about addition as more and more cats appear, and encourages them to compare quantities as Mama, who wants only one cat, figures how many cats is too many. The story also gives children the chance to think about how many eyes, ears, and paws there are for the ten cats in the story. And later in the story, as the cats are adopted by others, children have a chance to think about subtraction.

The story and the activities that follow help reinforce skills and build children's number sense. Because physical materials can be useful for learning, collect ten pennies for your child to use for some of the activities. Be curious about your child's reasoning and have fun exploring math together!

—Marilyn Burns

You'll find tips and suggestions for guiding the activities whenever you see a box like this!

Retelling the Story

Get 10 pennies to help you keep track of the cats in the story.

Mama is happy with Maxie, the one cat the family has. Put a penny on the first cat in the box.

But then five kittens howl at the door. Put five pennies on the next five cats. How many cats are there now? What are the kittens' names?

The pennies go on the cats in order from left to right, the same way we read and write. Your child should put the first penny on the first cat in the first row and fill up that row before starting on the next row.

Next, the neighbor's cats, Whiskers and Sam, move in. Put two pennies on the next two cats. How many cats are there now?

One day, a stray cat named Cat Fish jumps into the girl's backpack. Show this by putting a penny on the next cat on page 36. How many cats are there now?

Then Scooty scoots through the door. Put on another penny. Now you should have a penny on every cat. How many cats are there now?

"Ten cats is too many!" Mama says. So the girl puts up signs everywhere.

Mrs. Minnow takes one cat. Take off one penny. How many cats are there now?

The new neighbor takes two cats. Take off two more pennies. How many cats are there now?

> When removing the pennies, your child may not want to take them off in reverse order, but may be interested in figuring out which penny represents which specific cat. This is fine.

The Wilson triplets take three cats. Take off three more pennies. How many cats are there now?

A farmer takes two cats. Take off two more pennies. How many cats are there now?

A truck driver takes one cat. Take off one penny. How many cats are there now?

Why do you think Mama is happy now?

Then Maxie had four kittens. How many cats is that? What do you think Mama said?

How Many More or Less?

This is a game for two people.

Write the numbers from 1 to 10 on slips of paper and put them into a paper bag. Draw out one slip and put that many pennies on the cats on page 36. (Remember to start at the top and go from left to right.)

Draw out another slip and tell the other player how many pennies you must put on or take off so that the number of pennies matches your new number. Try it to see if your idea was right.

Now the other person takes a turn, drawing out a slip, figuring out how many pennies to add or subtract, and then doing it. When you've used up all the slips, put them back in the bag and play again.

Telling the Story with Number Sentences

You can write some of the sentences in the story with numbers instead of words. For example, when the new neighbor takes Whiskers and Sam to help her sort balls of yarn, the story says: "Two cats taken away from nine is seven." You can write that sentence with numbers: $9 - 2 = 7$.

Match the sentences from the story with the number sentences.

Five kittens and our cat Maxie add up to six.

Two old cats and five kittens and our cat Maxie add up to eight.

One stray cat and two old cats and five kittens and our cat Maxie add up to nine.

One cat taken away from ten is nine.

Three cats taken away from seven is four.

One cat taken away from two is one.

$7 - 3 = 4$

$1 + 2 + 5 + 1 = 9$

$5 + 1 = 6$

$2 - 1 = 1$

$10 - 1 = 9$

$2 + 5 + 1 = 8$

Ears, Eyes, Tails, and Paws

Look at pages 16 and 17. What does the story say about 10 cats being in the house? With 10 cats, why are there 20 cat eyes, 10 tails, 20 ears, and 40 paws?

Cat Riddles

If there are 20 cats, how many tails are there?

If there are 8 cats, how many eyes do they have all together?

If there are 5 cats, how many paws and tails do they have all together?

How many ears do 12 cats have all together?

How many paws and tails do 10 cats have all together?

When 6 cats are in the house, how many paws are there?

How many paws do 5 cats have all together?

How many paws and tails do 5 cats have all together?

How many ears do 7 cats have all together?

> Do as many of these riddles as interest your child. If your child needs help, drawing or using the pennies for cats may help. If your child needs harder problems, make the numbers larger.